CHOICES IN CHILDBEARING

CHOICES IN CHILDBEARING

WHEN DOES FAMILY PLANNING BECOME POPULATION CONTROL?

by *Robert Whelan*

Preface by Baroness Elles

"The central issue in population policy is whether the
number of children people may have should be decided
by individuals and families or politicians and
international civil servants"

Professor Lord Bauer
"Population Growth : Curse or Blessing ?"

Published by the Committee on Population and the Economy
London 1992

ISBN 0 946680 42 6

Book production by Crowley Esmonde Ltd, London
Typeset by Goodfellow & Egan Ltd, Cambridge
Printed by St Edmundsbury Press, Bury St Edmunds, Suffolk

Contents

Preface

The Third Committee of the United Nations General Assembly concerned with human rights topics has many women delegates from both developing and developed countries. I had the honour to be the United Kingdom delegate to the U.N. in 1972, a time when the question of population control was becoming divisive between the developed and the developing countries.

Developed countries were viewed with suspicion as threatening to force the developing countries to keep down the size of their populations for the benefit of the richer parts of the world.

Many colleagues – and I am pleased to say friends – among the African, Asian and Latin American delegations recognised that there were two entirely separate political concepts: the first, population control, which aimed to keep human numbers down because of the alleged threat of a population explosion; the second, the possibility for women, particularly in the developing countries, to have the opportunity to learn about family planning methods which would enable them as individuals to be able to make their own decisions as to the size of their families.

The good relations built up in the Third Committee at that time have been undermined by the apparently deliberate fusing of the two issues.

This study by Robert Whelan is of the greatest importance in identifying the fundamental difference between the two issues and will undoubtedly contribute to a better understanding and relationship between peoples.

Diana Elles

Whose Choice?

"Family planning begins and ends with individual couples choosing when to have children"

Malcolm Potts, Family Health International[1]

The assumption that the world is overpopulated is one of those things which 'everyone knows'. There has been such widespread agreement, in the media and amongst public policy makers, that the planet is threatened by a 'population explosion', and that we in the West should do something about it, that any expression of doubt on the issue is akin to claiming membership of the flat earth society.

It comes as a surprise to most people to learn that much of the serious academic research which has been carried out in the last 25 years into the effects of population growth has called into question the 'population explosion' hypothesis. Economists, social scientists and statisticians like Simon Kuznets, Julian Simon, Jacqueline Kasun, Colin Clark and Lord Bauer have questioned the supposed link between population growth and poverty, famine, unemployment and other problems.

However, since Western governments were persuaded in the mid 1960s to start putting money into population control programmes, a great industry has grown up. Tens of thousands of people are now employed worldwide in devising and administering programmes to reduce population growth. The level of funding runs into hundreds of millions of dollars annually. Chairs of population studies have been endowed at leading universities where professors are paid to do nothing except argue for population control.

In such a situation it will be easily understood that attempts to broaden the population debate will be fiercely and effectively resisted. For many people, there is too much at stake. As a result, this volume of research which contradicts the popular assumptions is seldom referred to in 'official' population publications.

However, there is an even more effective way of silencing debate on the issue. The population lobbyists claim that they only want to provide family planning services which will enable women around the world to control their fertility. The stated intention is to increase freedom of choice for women and to improve the state of women's health.

Those who oppose population programmes are therefore cast in the unenviable role of being against women's rights. This is not a mantle which many people are rushing to assume. The population lobbyists have been so successful in deflecting criticism in this way that most debates concerning opposition to population control have been confined to discussion of the Catholic Church's teaching on artificial contraception, and perhaps the role of women under Islam.

It is the argument of this monograph that the public have been misled concerning the nature and impact of population control programmes on parents, particularly women, in the developing countries. This has been achieved by distorting the use of the term 'family planning' until it ceases to represent what we would understand by it in the rich nations of the West.

Family planning, in its true sense, is a fundamentally different concept to population control.

Family planning is the decision taken by couples, in the light of their own beliefs and circumstances, as to the number and spacing of their own children.

Population control is the decision taken by governments or other agencies that couples should have no more than a certain number of children, followed by measures to enforce this.

Family planning and population control are not, as some like to make out, only different in degree. They are fundamentally opposed to each other, because family planning increases freedom of choice for the individual, while population control restricts it.

Family planning, in its true sense, is not controversial. No one – not even the Catholic Church – disputes that it is the right of parents to plan their own families. There may be disputes about the methods to be used – for example, whether abortion should be regarded as a method of family planning – but the principle is unchallenged.

Handing decisions about fertility to government planners is another matter. There is now no doubt that population control programmes have resulted in the widespread coercion of couples, sometimes involving the use of physical force, to ensure that they have fewer children than they would have wished.

How can this have come about in the name of freedom of choice? When looking at population programmes we have to ask ourselves, who is making the choices? The parents? The governments of the countries they live in? The governments of other countries? Or supra-national bodies like the World Bank and the United Nations?

The study of the way in which population programmes actually work should raise the most profound concern amongst those who care about human rights and, in particular, the welfare of women.

CHAPTER ONE

Who's Been Planning My Family?

"The things that make family planning acceptable are the very things that make it ineffective for population control. By stressing the right of parents to have the number of children they want, it evades the basic question of population policy, which is how to give societies the number of children they need"[1]

Kingsley Davis, Director of International Population and Urban Research, University of California, 1967

Fear of global population growth is now so universal that it is difficult to remember how recently this reaction set in.

No one thought very much about global population until after the Second World War. Prior to that the only interest in population concerned national statistics, and it is worth remembering that for most of mankind's history population growth has been regarded as a positive asset to a society in terms of security.

However, in 1952 the International Planned Parenthood Federation was founded at a meeting in Bombay, comprising eight national family planning bodies. These included the British Family Planning Association and Planned Parenthood Federation of America. In the same year the Population Council was founded in New York by John D Rockefeller III. Both organisations were committed to spreading alarm about the consequences of population growth, and to pressing for population control policies.

In its early years the population control movement was privately funded from the capacious pockets of some of the richest men and the richest private foundations on earth – the Rockefellers, the Ford Foundation, the millionaire Hugh Moore and others. At the time governments regarded fertility control as far too controversial for public support.

These reservations had disappeared by the mid-1960s in the face of an increasingly hysterical campaign to arouse fear of population growth, based at that time largely on predictions of mass famines which were envisaged as a result of populations outgrowing their resource base.

The 'population explosion' or 'population bomb' had by then become the principal day-of-doom story for the media. The emotive language which was used and the wild predictions which were seriously reported went almost unparalleled for silliness and extremism until the peak of AIDS hysteria in the media in the mid-1980s.

In this increasingly over-wrought atmosphere, some of the leading advocates of population control began to fear that the methods they were proposing to deal with 'overpopulation' would not be adequate to the task. Making family planning available to all couples throughout the world might be a noble idea, but would it work fast enough? And what if – horror of horrors – people in the developing countries proved to be so backward that they actually *wanted* large families? In other words, what would have to follow if birth control technology were made available, but nobody wanted to use it?

One of the most striking and startling attempts to get to grips with this dilemma was made by American population guru Kingsley Davis. In an article in *Science* in 1967 he berated his colleagues in the population control movement for assuming that all they had to do was to make birth control available, and then birthrates would go down. He argued that for many women large families appeared desirable; therefore they would not accept the proffered means of reducing the number of their children. Davis was clear that family planning would not serve in these circumstances:

"Suppose a woman does not want to use *any* contraceptive until after she has had four children. This is the type of question that is seldom raised in the family planning literature . . . Her attitude is construed as due to ignorance and 'cultural values', and the policy deemed necessary to change it is 'education'. No compulsion can be used, because the movement is committed to free choice"[2].

Davis proposed a much more radical approach. He argued that as "the conditions that cause births to be wanted or unwanted are beyond the control of family planning . . . the social structure and economy must be changed before a deliberate reduction in the birth rate can be achieved"[3].

Even more controversially, given the time of writing, he performed the birth control equivalent of 'coming out of the closet' and revealed a startling hidden agenda:

"Changes basic enough to affect motivation for having children would be changes in the structure of the family, in the position of women and in the sexual mores"[4].

He proposed the following means of achieving this goal:

". . . the government could pay people to permit themselves to be sterilised; all costs of abortion could be paid by the government; a substantial fee could be charged for a marriage license; a 'child tax' could be levied . . . governments . . . could . . . cease taxing single persons more than married ones; stop giving parents special tax exemptions; abandon income tax policy that discriminates against couples when the wife works; stop giving parents special tax exemptions . . . stop awarding public housing on the basis of family size . . . women could be required to work outside the home, or compelled by circumstances to do so. If, at the same time, women were paid as well as men and given equal educational and occupational opportunities . . . many women would develop interests that would compete with family interests"[5].

And so on. The startling thing about Davis' list, which would have seemed shocking at a time when abortion was widely regarded as killing and when the state was expected to support the institutions of marriage and the family, is the number of proposals which have been implemented in Western societies. We now know that Davis was right in his fundamental assumption: that the de-stabilising of the traditional family and the promotion of 'alternative' family structures and sex-roles leads to a very low birthrate. It is well known that the populations of most Western nations, which could be said to broadly conform to Davis' blueprint for an anti-child society, have had fertility rates which have been below replacement levels for several decades.

It is equally clear that, if it were possible actually to change the cultures of developing countries in order to make them more like our Western cultures, incorporating our views of relationships and sexuality, the birth rates of these countries would come down.

Realising this, the international population cartel took Davis' ideas and ran with them.

In 1969 Frederick Jaffe, Vice President of Planned Parenthood/World Population, prepared a memorandum for Bernard Berelson, President of the Population Council, listing measures to reduce fertility. The chart he drew up, which is reproduced in the Appendix on pages 54–55, was clearly based on Kingsley Davis' article for *Science*. Berelson, in turn, used it as the basis for a speech, ominously entitled *Beyond Family Planning*, which he delivered to the Population Conference in Dacca in 1969. Berelson adopted Jaffe's proposals and added some of his own.

Berelson set himself the target of reducing birthrates in the developing countries by half in the following two decades. He listed a variety of means which he considered had been "responsibly suggested" for achieving this goal, dividing them into voluntary and involuntary (i.e. forced) methods of fertility control.

The involuntary methods included sterilisation of all females by means of time-capsule contraceptives, reversible only after government approval; licenses to have children ("the unit certificate might be the 'deci-child' and

5

accumulation of ten of these units by purchase, inheritance or gift would permit a woman in maturity to have one legal child"); the compulsory sterilisation of men with three or more children; and the addition of a sterilising agent to the water supply ("substance now unknown, but believed the be available for field testing after 5–15 years of research").

Berelson addressed the ethical questions raised by these policies, and came to the conclusion that it all depends upon the seriousness with which one views the population problem:

> ". . . the worse the problem, the more one is willing to 'give up' in ethical position in order to attain 'a solution' ".

He also raises the interesting question of "what weight should be given to the opportunities of the next generation as against the ignorance, the prejudices, or the preferences of the present one?"[6]

Once again, it is notable that many of Berelson's proposals, including those under the 'involuntary' heading, have been put into effect in population programmes at different times, as we shall see later. The proposal to add sterilising agents to the water supply, which is perhaps the most drastic, is not yet known to have been tried out, but the possiblity of wiping out the fertility of whole communities by a single simple measure has haunted populations apparatchiks ever since.

In 1963 N C Wright, the Deputy Director General of the U.N. Food and Agriculture Organisation, was proposing the addition of a sterilising agent to salt[7], and as recently as 1990 Sir Graham Hills, Principal of Strathclyde University, was advocating the addition of a "heat resistant contraceptive" to milled cereals to render populations infertile. Those wishing to have children would have to fast for a week for fertility to return[8].

Whether or not these techniques of involuntary medication have ever been put into practice by population controllers is impossible to prove, but we do know that the people of some third world countries take their government's commitment to population control seriously enough to fear it. In 1986 the Kenyan government was infuriated by the widespread refusal of schoolchildren to drink their milk because of rumours that the government had put 'family planning' into it. In some schools children hid when medical teams arrived to vaccinate them, assuming that they were going to be rendered infertile[9].

Both Frederick Jaffe and Bernard Berelson were extremely influential figures in the population control movement, administering multi-million dollar budgets and enjoying easy access to the media. Their views had the impact of policy decisions for many of their fellow lobbyists for population control.

However, the increasing brutal and explicit calls for 'involuntary' techniques of fertility control, coupled with the the interference in other countries' cultures, provoked a backlash.

In 1974 the United Nations organised its first big international conference on population in Bucharest. The intention was to bring together representatives of the nations of the world to agree publicly to do something about population growth. As birthrates in the developed countries were already low and falling rapidly, it was clear that the real target of the conference's policies would be the developing countries.

However, the conference organisers were astonished when one Third World delegation after another stood up and attacked population control as a manifestation of Western imperialism. They demanded to know why their people should have fewer children in imitation of the Western model when they had not enjoyed the economic growth which had accompanied the falling birthrates in the West. "Development is the best contraceptive" was their slogan, meaning that when they were as prosperous as Westerners, they would have Western-style small families. The World Population Plan of Action (WPPA) issued by the conference had to be drastically altered to remove all references to population targets. Third World sensibilities were running high.

The population controllers learned their lesson. If they intended to continue reducing fertility in Third World countries they would have to change their approach. Everything would have to be couched in terms which disguised the real motives for the programmes.

"THE NORMAL OPERATION OF U.S. COMMERCIAL INTERESTS"

In December 1974 the National Security Council of the United States completed a study entitled *Implications of Worldwide Population Growth for U.S. Security and Overseas Interests*. It was also known as the National Security Study Memorandum 200 or NSSM 200[10].

The Memorandum expressed the gravest fears that the "political consequences of current population factors in the LDCs (less developed countries)" might create "political or even national security problems for the U.S." (page 10 introduction).

These "population factors" – i.e. rapid population growth – were expected to be a cause of civil unrest which could threaten the supply of resources necessary to the U.S. economy, particularly if growing populations were to demand a greater share of the world's wealth. It was also feared that large numbers of young people in developing countries might form an effective protest movement against the perceived domination of their countries by foreign interests like multi-national corporations.

For these and other reasons the Memorandum advised that:

". . . the President and the Secretary of State treat the subject of population growth control as a matter of paramount importance" (page 18).

Furthermore the endorsement of the Memorandum's recommendations in National Security Decision Memorandum 314 (NSDM 314), issued in November 1975, included "a global target of replacement fertility levels by the year 2000".

However, the authors of the Memorandum had the outrage expressed by Third World nations at Bucharest fresh in their minds. They therefore made the following recommendation:

"The U.S. can help to minimize charges of an imperialist motivation behind its support of population activities by repeatedly asserting that such support derives from a concern with: (a) the right of the individual to determine freely and responsibly the number and spacing of children . . . and (b) the fundamental social and economic development of poor countries" (page 115).

The language of these specious defences had been borrowed from the World Population Plan of Action agreed at Bucharest. The Third World nations had been more interested in talking about their economic growth (or lack of it) than their population growth, and the WPPA had recognised "the basic human right of all couples and individuals to decide freely and responsibly the number and spacing of their children".

This is the way in which population control can be made to look like family planning. Henry Kissinger and the other authors of NSSM 200 recognised full well that population control was cheaper than development. The Memorandum noted "how much more efficient expenditures for population control might be than [would be funds for] raising production through direct investments in additional irrigation and power projects and factories" (page 53).

The authors of the Memorandum also recognised that the U.S. government might be open to criticism owing to the fact that assistance to health programmes in the Third World had been falling at the same time that expenditures on population control programmes had been rising. They therefore proposed integrating population with health programmes, so that expenditures on both could be mixed up, whilst arguing that it was all being done for the sake of the health of mothers and their children (page 177).

It is clear that, for the population control lobby, nothing had changed except the rhetoric. The interests pursued were to be those of the developed nations: the language used would refer to women's health and the right to space children.

The significance of this policy decision can hardly be overestimated. It provided a brilliantly successful technique for meddling with the fertility of Third World women without incurring charges of imperialism and unwarranted interference in the affairs of another country. It was adopted throughout the population control movement, with the result that, from the mid-1970s to the present day, they have argued their case almost exclusively on the grounds of protecting the health of women around the world.

It is true there have been some rogue voices, but these have been quickly silenced in the larger population bureaucracies. In 1977 Dr Reimert Ravenholt, the Director of the Office of Population for the U.S. Agency for International Development, told a journalist that he aimed for the sterilisation of a quarter of the world's fertile women in order to secure "the normal operation of U.S. commercial interests around the world"[11]. The statement drew a good deal of criticism and appears to have been made in an unguarded moment. It was certainly never repeated, and no other similarly blunt statements of intent have emerged from mainstream population groups.

CHAPTER TWO

Culture Vultures

As Kinglsey Davis pointed out in his article for Science in 1967, making birth control available will not, in itself, bring down birthrates because people will not necessarily use it. The desire for small families which is almost universal in Western, industrial cultures is not replicated in the Third World. On the contrary, there is still a marked preference for large families, for all sorts of cultural, social and religious reasons, across large parts of the globe.

As Sally Mugabe explained in *Popline*:

> "For a [Zimbabwean] woman, bearing and rearing children is the primary source of status in the family and the community. The larger number of children a woman has, the higher the status she enjoys"[1]

This recalls the story, often told at population gatherings, of the African leader who began a speech to his countrymen about the dangers of overpopulation with the words "My people, our birth rate is so high that our numbers will double in only 25 years and . . ." The rest of the speech was drowned out by wild cheering.

This humorous anecdote is validated by serious scientific studies. The Washington-based Information Project for Africa has documented the way in which population controllers have had to face up to the fact that not only is there virtually no demand for their services in Africa: there is a very strong cultural opposition to the Western notion of family limitation. According to the IPFA Report *Unconventional Warfare and the Theory of Competetive Reproduction*[2]:

> "A study conducted between 1987 and 1989 in Senegal to determine attitudes toward modern contraception found 'zero per cent use of modern methods' among 580 women surveyed[3]. Similar group research in Burkina Faso revealed that although all but 17 per cent of women questioned were knowledgeable of Western birth control, the majority still believed that the number of children born to a couple should be 'up to God'[4] . . .

> "Even the AID (U.S. Agency for International Development) project plan for a massive $100 million birth control campaign in Nigeria conceded that while actual fertility in that country is high – roughly 6.5 children per family – the desired number of children per woman is considerably higher,

at an estimated 8.5[5]. Actual fertility in Benin has been estimated at 6.5 children per woman, while desired fertility is 7.6; in Cote d'Ivoire actual fertility is 6.6, compared to desired fertility of 8.4; in Mauretania, average children per family number 6.0, while desired fertility is 8.8; and in Zimbabwe the respective numbers were 6.0 and 7.0[6].

"In one of the most comprehensive studies ever done about cultural barriers to birth control among Africans – part of a published World Bank symposium – John C Caldwell and Pat Caldwell reviewed over 100 sources, including anthropological research dating to the 1930s and works by major African scholars. They concluded that the preference for high fertility in Africa involves every level of conscious and subconscious thinking. The Caldwells wrote:

'The mother of many children is regarded as a special person and is respected by all, whereas women with small families were pitied and ridiculed . . . There is a deeply ingrained idea that normal men and women should continue to beget children throughout their fecund years . . . Indeed, the Edo of Nigeria address God as the "bringer of children" . . . African governments have given either no leadership or uncertain leadership to family planning programs . . . The real problem is that politicians, civil servants and political activists all feel that the programs may run counter to the basic spiritual beliefs and emotions of African society'."[7]

The special problems involved in reducing fertility in Africa have long been apparent to the population controllers. According to Population Council senior associate Rousdi A Henin, birth control campaigns in other parts of the developing world have been able "to bolster existing demand by creating awareness that the commodity exists, showing how, and when it can be used and where it can be found". But in Africa, according to Henin, the situation is:

". . . culturally, historically and socio-economically different. What is needed in Africa is to change cultural attitudes to family size. Here it is not a question of 'strengthening' demand . . . but literally to create demand for a commodity which is culturally unacceptable at all levels of the community"[8].

The realisation that, in order to change birthrates, it will first be necessary to change cultural conditioning, is widely taken as read throughout the population control lobby. According to the World Bank's 1984 report *Population Change & Economic Development*:

". . . use of contraception depends not only on accessibility and cost, but also on how intensely a couple wishes to avoid a birth"[9].

Quite. And according to Barber Conable, President of the World Bank,:

"We need to, first, ensure that men and women desire smaller families"[10].

Just how this change in "desire" can be brought about is a question which has occupied the population planners for many years. Between 1984 and 1988 the Population Council, using funding from the U.S. Agency for International Development, published a series of studies on 'fertility determinants'. The aim was to examine the cultural and socio-economic factors which influence attitudes towards fertility control. The reports were analysed by Jean M Guilfoyle of the Population Research Institute in Baltimore in an article for the *Population Research Institute Review*[11]:

"The report titled *The Proximate Determinants of Fertility in High Fertility Countries* (September 1988) advised that *'the meaningful approach to fertility reduction will be to discourage favorable attitudes towards large families and attempt the idealization of small to medium family size. This approach'* it added *'will be more effective in lowering the demand for children than the offer of contraception within marriage'* . . .

"Another report in the series, written by Robert A LeVine and published in September of 1984 . . . disclosed that patterns of maternal behavior are heavily validated by local moral codes, religious and medical beliefs, and culturally organized 'common sense'. But, LeVine noted, a *'basic premise of the research'* was that significant *'adaptive changes in maternal behavior'* can come about rather quickly – *'sometimes within a generation, sometimes in two or more generations'*[12].

"The 'fertility determinant' series was intended to present information upon which policies might be based, and not to specifically recommend any particular policy approach. Nonetheless, some of its findings strongly suggest that any serious attempt to impose population control on high-fertility societies might require an organized and deliberate attempt to undermine religious institutions, to transform local economies, and to develop patterns of consumption that compete with child-rearing.

"One of these research papers *Causes of Fertility Decline in South India* by John C Caldwell, P H Reddy and Pat Caldwell, found that these factors had been instrumental to a decline in birthrates in several southern regions of India[13]. . . .

"*'Changes in relationships within the family, in arrangements of marriages, in availabiity of jobs and education, and in the perception of the economic value of children all helped alter South Indian society during the past two decades'* the authors wrote. They advised that exposure to what was called 'English ways' – changes in language, secularization, and exposure to Western entertainment – had a negative impact on the desire for large families . . .

"Additionally the researchers found *'secularization has been invading such areas as perceptions of the cause and cure of illness . . . the duration of postnatal sexual abstinence and lactation, and the acceptance of fertility control'* . . .

"In conclusion the report finds that all these changes have *'moved the society towards family planning'* – primarily sterilization. *'Whatever uncertainties family planning members may have about sterilization is compensated for by the certainty of the family planning workers and the government that gains will come from limiting family size'*

"This combination of factors – secularization, new concepts of health care, the emerging view that children are a financial liability to their parents, and the government-imposed perception that *'gains will come from limiting family size'* – invariably lead to the idea that children are to be, at least in some circumstances, 'unwanted'. Thus, with or without the legalization of abortion, social pressure and personal incentives to reject pregnancy become commonplace".

The Population Council's *Fertility Determinants Research Notes* did not achieve widespread publicity: they were intended primarily for circulation within the various groups which comprise the population lobby. Furthermore, as Jean Guilfoyle points out, they made no specific policy recommendations. However, they are of the greatest significance in that they reveal the awareness amongst population activists of the extent to which the cultures of other countries would need to be modified if their birthrates were to be brought into line with Western norms.

We shall now look at the methods which have been used to promote what the authors of these reports described as "English ways" in the developing world.

13

CHAPTER THREE

The Media Blitz

When asked how cultural barriers to fertility control programmes could be broken down, most population lobbyists would answer "through education".

However, 'population education' would be more accurately described as 'anti-natalist propaganda', because it lacks essential elements of good educational practice. It does not present information impartially; it does not try to assist students to evaluate between the claims of competing theories; and, most importantly, it does not encourage people to think for themselves. On the contrary, the aim of 'population education' is to make people – particularly Third World parents – think like white Western liberals.

In his 1967 essay for *Science* Kinglsey Davis had described population education as consisting of "movie strips, posters, comic books, public lectures, interviews and discussions"[1]. In the context of our modern world of instant mass communications his views seem quaint.

Anti-natalist propaganda today still involves the comics and the posters, but the major thrust in altering attitudes towards family size now comes through the broadcast media.

In 1989 *People*, the magazine of the International Planned Parenthood Federation, published an article by Phyllis Piotrow describing an international conference on Entertainment for Social Change which had been sponsored by three American organisations: the Population Communication Services project of the John Hopkins University, the Annenberg School of Communications at the University of Southern California, and the Centre for Population Options.

Phyllis Piotrow was already the doyenne of the population/showbusiness nexus. Together with her colleague Patrick Coleman in the John Hopkins University Population Communication Project, she had been successfully using media outlets to promote population programmes throughout the 1980s. Their first big success came with the promotion of a birth control message in a pop record by Mexican teen idols Tatiana and Johnny. The record, *Cuando Estemos Juntos* had reached number one in the charts in 1986 and went platinum. The John Hopkins team followed this with a similar hit record in the Philippines by Lea Salonga.

Another 'success' for the John Hopkins team, which is funded by the U.S. Agency for International Development, was a Turkish campaign targetted at

14

married women which was followed by the insertion of 250,000 IUDs. "What we've shown is [these campaigns] will change the behaviour of some people" said Ms Piotrow[2].

The conference on Entertainment and Social Change was the brain child of Piotrow's partner at John Hopkins University Patrick Coleman, and coined the ominous term 'enter-educate'. Some of the participants described their 'successes' in 'enter-educating':

JAMAICA: The radio soap opera Naisberry Street, supported by the local IPPF affiliate, uses a family planning clinic as the location for some scenes

INDIA: Family planning was also promoted in Hum Log, an Indian soap opera

NIGERIA: Elizabeth Okaro, a TV producer working in conjunction with the John Hopkins University team, had produced a variety show with family planning skits which helped to triple attendances at local family planning clinics.

A panel of researchers at the conference confirmed that "good entertainment wins people's attention, keeps them interested and sets up role models that people will copy"[3].

This has certainly been the experience of others involved with 'enter-education'. In Egypt President Mubarak became so worried about overpopulation that he himself took control of the population control programme for his country in the mid-1980s. The government tried a variety of methods to persuade its citizens to limit births without much success, until an advertising man came up with the idea for a series of four-minute TV dramas called *Dr Karima* in which a popular actress plays a doctor dispensing advice to patients:

> "The soap operas . . . are praised by health officials for breaking down the traditional social, economic and religious obstacles to family planning in a mainly Islamic nation where many influential local imams still teach that curbing family size contravenes the will of God. 'The media campaign played the first and main role in the success we have established in reducing the rate of the population growth', Maher Mahran, co-ordinator of the population council, explained"[4].

TARGET NIGERIA

The country which appears to have been singled out as the target for the biggest blitz of Western-sponsored anti-natalist propaganda is Nigeria.

In 1986 the U.S. Agency for International Development awarded the John Hopkins University Population Communication Service (JHU-PCS) $30 million for a 5 year campaign of "significant and sustained" communication in sub-Saharan Africa using "culturally appropriate" messages to increase the "level of requests for services" at family planning clinics[5].

A further $15 million was awarded specifically for work in Nigeria, under a contract which required the John Hopkins team to "be materially instrumental in bringing about a situation in which 80 per cent of the eligible population aged 15 – 45 are knowledgeable about family planning concepts"[6].

Under the terms of the contract, JHU-PCS were to produce "at least 3,000 television, radio, film and folk media programs and spots, and newspaper and magazine inserts in at least five languages, and will effect their dissemination by Nigeria's 22 television and 35 radio stations, by its 19 daily and 18 weekly newspapers, and by its 9 major nationwide magazines".

A variety of methods were detailed, including "exploiting fully traditional media, such as town criers, talking drums, dances, songs, drama troupes, and puppet shows . . . integrating family planning messages into existing popular radio and television series (variety shows and soap operas), and into newspaper and magazine sections".

The contract states that:

> "By December 21 1992 . . . it is expected that there will be a broad political and social constituency supportive of family planning policies and programs, that there will be significant attitudinal changes favoring smaller family norms, and that 80 per cent of the population aged 15–44 will be aware of modern contraception and its benefits".

As the percentage of the population using birth control was estimated to be only 3–4 percent at the start of the programme, this figure of 80 percent shows the scale of of the contract's aims. It was, however, reasonable to expect that the injection of these huge sums of money into the Nigerian communications industry, which is very small by Western standards, would have very considerable impact. In 1990 the U.S. Agency for International Development gave JHU-PCS a further $60 million.

One of the projects funded under the scheme was the production of two tracks promoting birth control for a record featuring popular singer King Sunny Ade. $350,000 was spent on producing and promoting the record and its accompanying video – a gigantic sum in the terms of the Nigerian recording business – but it seems that the sponsors went to considerable lengths to conceal the Western origins of the cash. Ade maintains that he did not understand that the ultimate source of the money was the U.S. government – through the Agency for International Development. This is probably true as USAID is not mentioned in his contract with the John Hopkins University, and even the involvement of the latter was to be kept very low key. The contract stipulates that apart from crediting JHU-PCS as the licensee of the songs on the record jacket, there was to be no further mention of John Hopkins University in promoting the record. Ade claims that he believed the inclusion of the two tracks promoting birth control on the record had been the idea of his wife, who sang with him, and that he had no idea that it was a part of any population programme.

According to the Information Project for Africa, which has carried out a detailed analysis of the JHU-PCS programme in Nigeria:

"The most frightening aspect of the Ade record case is the fact that it is but one of thousands of similar activities being funded in Nigeria through the John Hopkins program . . . it is therefore entirely possible that a large number of collaborators have been recruited without knowing either the source or the purpose of the activities for which they were paid. In that way, the John Hopkins population program and others that carry out similar missions for the U.S. government are able to gather intelligence about hundreds of people who can be paid to assist in foreign influence campaigns, even though many do so unknowingly"[7].

DOES IT MATTER?

According to Dr Halfdan Mahler, Secretary-General of the International Planned Parenthood Federation, his "vision for the 1990s" is that "by the year 2000 IPPF should be able to say that it has supported countries all over the world to have policies, mechanisms and infrastructures in place whereby every woman and man would find it difficult to escape being properly informed about planned and responsible parenthood"[8].

Given the sort of funds which are now flooding into Third World media outlets, courtesy of IPPF and other population organisations, this seems entirely within the bounds of possibility. Third World parents will be nagged, exhorted, lectured to and browbeaten by 'population education' in an attempt to 'motivate' them to have smaller families.

Does it really matter? After all, you can always turn off the television or radio. You don't have to read a particular newspaper.

The problems involved in avoiding government propaganda are much less significant in the West than they are in many Third World countries. For one thing, we are used to having access to a variety of radio and TV channels, and a range of newspapers reflecting different viewpoints. Even in countries where some outlets may be state controlled – like the BBC in the U.K. – these still have to compete with commercial rivals. The amount of time allocated to political messages will therefore be strictly limited. TV viewers in Britain have shown themselves to be so unwilling to watch even 10-minute party political broadcasts that the old rule decreeing that all channels had to broadcast them at the same time has been dropped. It is now relatively easy to avoid them altogether.

The situation in Third World countries is very different. The number of outlets for both broadcast and print media is much more limited. Furthermore, in many countries these are all either controlled by the state or subject to very strict censorship. People may therefore not have access to anything other than these official sources of information. To fill them with propaganda is to pervert the channels of communication.

There is another critical point to which Lord Bauer has drawn attention:

"In many Third World countries, especially in Asia and Africa, official information, advice and persuasion in practice often shade into coercion. In most of these societies people are more subject to authority than in the West. And especially in recent years, the incomes and prospects of many individuals have come to depend heavily on official favours"[9].

We must now look at the ways in which official population programmes "shade into coercion".

CHAPTER FOUR

Sticks & Carrots

Population control groups realised long ago that they would face intractable problems if they maintained their support for 'freedom of choice' for the individual, and the individual wanted a large family.

In response to this dilemma they devised a system of incentives and disincentives. This can be more simply expressed as sticks and carrots, that is to say, bribes for those who tow the government's line on family size and punishments for parents who have more than the permitted number of children.

At its simplest level this involves cash payments to 'acceptors' of family planning – usually sterilisation, in this context. In Vietnam a woman receives 20 kg of rice and two weeks holiday if an IUD is inserted, 100 kg of rice and lighter duties at work for a sterilisation [1].

In Bangladesh 'acceptors' of sterilisation receive *Taka* 175, which is the equivalent of a week's wages for a rural labourer. In addition, female patients receive a *saree* and men a *lungi*. Although this may not seem like a great deal, the advantages would be more obvious to an unemployed and destitute parent. A report published in *Studies in Family Planning* in 1991 concluded that the payments were sufficient to influence behaviour:

> "The profit may seem far too trivial to act as an inducement for a lifetime decision . . . (but) the possiblity cannot be dismissed when the sum involved is set against the extreme poverty and daily struggle to survive of much of the population"[2].

The suspicion that the financial incentives may act as a pressure on the 'acceptors' is confirmed by the fact that there was a dramatic increase in vasectomies following an increase in the incentive payments in 1983, and that a "seasonal peak" in sterilisations occurs each year to coincide with "the lean inter-harvest period, when employment is low and money short"[3].

The rewards offered to the clerical caste are proportionately larger. In August 1990 Bangladesh's National Council for Population Control approved incentive payments to civil servants which would include a retirement lump sum equivalent to one year's salary for those with only one child, and the equivalent of six months salary for those with two. All taxpayers would receive a rebate of 15% for those with one child and 10% for those with two[4].

19

Incentives do not stop at cash payments. In their report *Food, Saris and Sterilization*, Hilary Standing and Betsy Hartmann revealed that emergency food aid which had been donated following the 1984 floods in Bangladesh had been given to women on condition that they agreed to be sterilised. Following the operation, the woman would receive a certificate signed by the family planning officer which would entitle her to a sari, money and wheat[5].

The 1984 World Bank Report *Population Change & Economic Development* contained an extensive discussion of the use of incentives in population programmes[6]. Here are some of the examples quoted:

TANZANIA: Working women in the government service are allowed paid maternity leave only once every three years

SINGAPORE: Income tax relief available for first three children only. Paid maternity leave for first two pregnancies only. Children from smaller families given priority in school admissions. State housing allocated without regard to family size.★

KOREA: Free medical care and education allowances to two-child families provided one of the parents has been sterilised.

THAILAND: Technical assistance in farm production and marketing is made available to contraceptive users. "Rates of contraceptive use have risen to as high as 80% in some villages that receive, or hope to receive, the benefits of this program."

INDIA: Women working on tea plantations received an extra day's pay for every month they were not pregnant.

Some of incentives listed by the World Bank verge on the farcical. For example, contracepting villagers in Thailand have been allowed to use a "family planning bull" to service their cattle[7]. The fact that calves are regarded as an asset whilst babies are regarded as a liability demonstrates Lord Bauer's contention that calculations of national income per head of population are a flawed method for measuring the wellbeing of a community:

> "The birth of a child immediately reduces income per head for the family and also for the country as a whole. The death of the same child has the opposite effect. Yet, for most people, the first event is a blessing, and the second a tragedy. Ironically the birth of a child is registered as a reduction in national income per head, while the birth of a farm animal shows up as an improvement"[8].

★ *The population programme in Singapore has subsequently been thrown into reverse to encourage more births*

Even more insidious than incentives to individuals are the incentives which are offered to whole communities which achieve family planning 'targets'. The system reached a peak in Indonesia where, under the direction of Western population agencies, the government developed the "village system" of family planning.

PEER GROUP PRESSURE IN INDONESIA

The World Bank Development Report for 1980 described how, in the province of Bali, the monthly village council meeting "begins with a roll call; each man responds by saying whether he and his wife are using contraceptives. Replies are plotted on a village map – prominently displayed"[9]. The central government sets "targets" for the number of "new acceptors" of contraception[10], and provides group rewards to villages which reach these targets. These may consist of increased food supplements, health services and other benefits[11], including public meeting halls, road repairs and clean water supply[12].

It is not difficult to imagine the sort of pressures which couples would come under if they did *not* want to participate in the government's population control programme. They would be the ones stopping their neighbours from obtaining extra food, or clean water. Peer pressure could easily become intolerable for them.

It is worth asking ourselves, how would we feel if our own governments made access to clean water and road building programmes contingent on the level of birth control practised by those living in our street or town? It seems unlikely that any Western government would survive the political fallout which would result from any such attempt to interfere in the most private areas of its citizens' lives. And yet we are happy to pay for such schemes in the developing world through our taxes which are used to fund the international population control lobby.

The Indonesian programme became a great favourite of the population controllers because, on its own terms, it worked. Fertility rates fell dramatically from 5.5 children per woman in 1970, before the government began its "vigorous family planning programme" to 4.3 in 1982[13]. In June 1988 President Suharto of Indonesia was presented with the United Nations Population Award "in recognition of his country's success in achieving a significant decline in fertility"[14]. The U.S. House Select Committee on Population recorded, without any apparent regret, that the "improvements" (i.e. the falling birthrates) "occurred in the absence of significant gains in the social and economic conditions of the vast majority of Indonesians"[15]. In other words, the prosperity which is supposed to attend reductions in the birthrates had not arrived.

21

Before leaving Indonesia, which is in many ways a textbook example of the violation of the individual's right to choose by government population programmes, we should mention a particularly nasty 'incentive' to family planning developed there. According to a report in *People*, the magazine of the International Planned Parenthood Federation, women in Padang Panjang, a Muslim farming community, have complained that their children cannot get their report cards from school unless they can produce their mother's identity card proving her involvement with the government's family planning programme[16]. This is a grotesque violation of the woman's right to privacy and the child's right to an education.

INCENTIVES FOR 'MOTIVATORS'

The use of incentives in birth control programmes does not end with the so-called 'acceptors' of family planning. Many schemes also involve financial inducements to the 'motivators' – the people who, by hook or by crook, get them to the clinics, and to the doctors who carry out the sterilisations or provide the contraception.

Ever since India became the first country in the world to adopt a population policy in 1952 it has been the testing ground for the development of every technique for population control. A TV documentary shown on Channel 4 called *Something Like A War* exposed the labyrinthine network of 'motivators' who press Indian men and women to 'accept' birth control, usually sterilisation[17]. This network involves not only the *patwaris* and civil servants engaged full-time on the population programme, but community workers, teachers and ration-shop owners. In their eagerness to get the maximum number of 'acceptors', or 'cases' to their credit they were outdoing each other with bribes to the people, and with lies about what the 'acceptors' could expect in exchange for their fertility:

Motivator

"When we come to con people . . . to agree to sterilisation we promise to solve their land problems or whatever. No one will do it for the government money. We tell them that if there's any work they want done on their land or any other assistance we promise to help and guide them. Sometimes the community worker, a teacher or a ration-shop keeper offers the 'case' a better deal and then the 'case' walks off with him"

Ration-Shop Keeper

"To get a 'case' we must give them money. We pay about 100 to 450 rupees on top of the government's 160 rupees. We brought in many 'cases' by adjusting the food ration supplies. There's a lot of pressure put on us to bring in 'cases' "[2]

Interviewer

"What sort of pressure?"

Ration-Shop Keeper

"To keep our shops we must bring in cases. If not, we'll lose our shops."

Two Women Who Have Been Sterilised

1st WOMAN: "They lie about the land, they promise you this and that, and when the operation's done they dump you.

2nd WOMAN: "Last year they said they'd give us a free house and 500 rupees. They didn't give us a thing."

Two Indian doctors wrote to *The Lancet* about the pressures under which medical staff were operating in order to keep up with the Indian government's sterilisation programme:

"Local authorities are under pressure to achieve set targets and the doctors are paid on a case basis . . . inducements (cash or otherwise) are routinely sanctioned to candidates for sterilisation, and the motivator is similarly rewarded; the organizational structure is insufficient, and informed consent is certainly not obtained. Many gynaecologists pride themselves on the number of sterilisations they do."[18]

The doctors reported many complications, some resulting from the lack of experience of the medical staff:

"One general surgeon describes how he had to rescue an inexperienced doctor looking for tubes in the opened urinary bladder on one occasion and in an opened loop of bowel on another . . . We can expect 4000 5000 ectopic pregnancies as a result of these procedures. Since most would arise in rural areas where blood transfusion and emergency services are inadequate, the resulting deaths would have to be set against deaths from unwanted pregnancies that were avoided"[19].

The casual attitude which is taken towards the health of women in these schemes was confirmed by women participating in the Channel 4 documentary *Something Like A War*. One woman described how her daughter developed very severe complications after being fitted with an IUD, but when she went back to the hospital the staff refused to remove it.

1st WOMAN: "It was causing problems – they should have taken it out. If you die it's just too bad – they don't care – it won't affect their lives".

2nd WOMAN: "They treat women's bodies as a game. The government wants the programme to go on, whether you live or die."

This callousness is the inevitable outcome of a population programme which sets targets and functions through an elaborate network of bribes or 'incentives'. People become 'cases' to be clocked up, not individuals whose treatment should relate to their own health needs. In spite of this the World Bank defends incentive payments to doctors and 'motivators' by claiming:

". . . they are meant not to increase demand for services but to improve supply"[20].

Whoever wrote that sentence had a very limited experience of real life.

The use of incentives is sometimes justified on the basis that, unless poor people can be compensated for their time and travelling expenses, they will not be able to come to the clinics. Travelling expenses might be justified under this heading, but not clothing and certainly not food allocations.

Also, it should be remembered that no incentives were required to promote health care programmes in the Third World like the innoculation programmes against smallpox and measles, which have had such a dramatic effect on mortality rates, particularly infant mortality. In those cases people readily came forward to participate because they could understand the advantages which would accrue to them. If they have to be pressured to take part in birth control programmes it may not necessarily be because they are stupid, selfish and irresponsible, as some members of the population lobby make out. It may be because they understand that the programmes are not in their best interests. Of course, the population controllers think they know better. But then, they always do.

CHAPTER FIVE

Piggy-Backing

What can the population controllers do if people really don't want to use birth control? One very effective answer is to link it to something they do want. As the World Bank report *Population Change and Economic Development* puts it:

"In communities where there is no apparent demand for family planning, it can be introduced jointly with services in greater demand"[1].

The obvious programme on which family planning can be piggy-backed is primary health care. This is logical and unobjectionable as long as participation remains voluntary. Unfortunately there is evidence to suggest that women feel that they must take the family planning in order to get the component which they really want.

A speaker at an international conference on health and family planning in Washington explained:

"Many field workers have found that when family planning programs are not integrated with health services it is difficult to sustain their initial impact[2]."

He illustrated his point by describing an extraordinary trial caried out by the United Nations Population Fund (UNFPA) and the U.S. Agency for International Development (USAID) in Bangladesh. Family planning had been made part of a health care project which also provided oral rehydration treatment (ORT) to mothers whose babies were suffering from diarrhoea. As diarrhoea is a major cause of infant mortality in the Third World, the offer of this treatment would have been a very strong incentive to women to use the family planning clinic.

The trial, of which the aim was to determine which combination of health care and birth control would produce the highest contraceptive prevalence rate, involved issuing some women with American produced oral rehydration packets, made from pre-mixed sugar and electrolyte salts, and other women with instruction in a simple alternative method using locally available salt and molasses. The women using this alternative method had no further need to attend the clinic for ORT.

The drop out rate from attendance at the family planning clinic was twice as high amongst women using the simple home remedy as it was amongst women using the USAID produced rehydration packets. This suggests that they were only visiting the family planning clinic in the first place because they wanted the oral rehydration treatment for their children, not because the wanted birth control[3].

Another technique developed by USAID in Bangladesh has been to send Community Health Workers literally to the doorsteps of targetted women to present a full range of birth control methods. According to a speaker at another international health conference:

"The regular presence of the CHW (Community Health Worker) at the villager's doorstep, her constant emphasis on family planning . . . have created the trust *as well as the pressure necessary* to persuade women to adopt contraception" (emphasis added)[4].

Even in developed countries poor people may be in awe of professional people, like doctors. In the developing countries, where the balance of power between government and governed is much more uneven, doctors who are employed on a government project may be in a position to mislead and intimidate their patients into 'accepting' certain sorts of treatment. This is particularly apparent where there are strong incentives to the doctor to maximise the number of his or her 'acceptors', coupled with penalites for failing to meet the targets. Under these conditions doctors may dispense with the nicer points of medical practice, like obtaining informed consent.

The Family Education Trust video *The Great Population Hoax*[5] includes disturbing testimonies from Third World doctors concerning the treatment of women under population control programmes:

Dr Mary Chore (Kenya)
"Recently I had a case where a woman had had a coil put in her. She had taken her sick child to the clinic and had also complained of abdominal pains. The doctor in that clinic just decided to put a coil in her without informing her what was happening. For the last two years she has not been able to conceive and herself and the husband are very concerned – they didn't know what was happening. They came to us, we started our investigations, only to find that she had a coil inside her for the last two years which she did not know was there"

Dr Marie Mascarenhas (India)
"I'm especially concerned about the coercion that goes on in some of the family planning programmes. A woman from a slum area who had gone in for a gynaecological check-up came out and received a small steel plaque, like a plate, which is very expensive normally and very useful to

an Indian woman. But this woman was intelligent and she knew that normally she's never given a gift when she comes out from a hospital and so she asked, 'Why is the gift being given to me?' And the woman said 'Today every woman who has a loop inserted gets this gift as an incentive'. But she said 'I never asked for a loop and I don't want a loop', and she was able to inform the other women who came out."

OTHER OPTIONS

Family planning can be piggy-backed onto a variety of other welfare projects as well as health care. Here are some inventive examples:

JAVA: Loans were made available to groups of women using family planning, on the grounds that women with fewer children have the opportunity to expand their earning capacity[6]

HONDURAS: The Family Planning Association includes the promotion of family planning in its community-based adult literacy programme[7]

THAILAND: The Population and Communication Development Association of Thailand (PDA) works with Singer Sewing Machine Co as part of a dressmaking project[8].

An article on the Indonesian government's population programme in *People*, the magazine of the International Planned Parenthood Federation, gave an insight into a particularly clever scheme to involve women from a Muslim community in 'family planning'. To overcome the resistance which these women had shown, the National Family Planning Co-ordinating Board organised small groups for monthly meetings. These groups included women who had previously refused 'family planning':

"For many months no one talked about family planning. The women received lessons in sewing and began to make school uniforms to sell to the village co-operative. They learned more about cooking and embroidery. Gradually the tutors introduced information about health and malnutrition – and from there is was only a short step to discussing the importance of delayed marriage and child-spacing. As a result, the programme has drawn an average of two new acceptors per month"[9].

In order to get some sort of perspective on the nature of these programmes, we should ask ourselves how we would react if our own government were to tie participation in, say, Youth Training Schemes or the Enterprise Initiative to 'acceptance' of family planning.

CHAPTER SIX

The Use of Force in India

"We must now act decisively and bring down the birth rate speedily. We should not hesitate to take steps which might be described as drastic. Some personal rights have to be kept in abeyance for the human rights of the nation"

Indira Ghandi 1976

Ever since the International Planned Parenthood Federation (IPPF) was founded in India in 1952, that country has occupied a special place in the attentions of the population controllers.

The Indian government became the first in the world to implement an official population policy in the same year, and since then almost every new idea in fertility control has been tried out there.

As Western population lobbyists became more and more alarmed at the ever increasing numbers of Indians being born, India was singled out for a determined campaign. John Lewis, head of the Indian office of the U.S. Agency for International Development, announced that he "would press [population] funds on the Indian government whether it wants them or not"[1].

Sterilisation has been the favoured means of fertility control in India, and the Indian programme is unusual in that it has been targetted heavily at men. In different states at different times almost everything, from jobs in the civil service to public housing and even licenses to run taxi firms, has been made dependent on the 'acceptance' of vasectomy.

Mass sterilisation camps were set up in Kerala in 1970 which, accompanied by a lot of ballyhoo and in a strangely carnival-type atmosphere, resulted in 15,005 vasectomies. The following year the figure was 62,913 vasectomies. As other districts tried to emulate these initial successes, newspapers began to publish scoreboards to show which areas were performing best in the sterilisation stakes. As Germaine Greer explains in her book *Sex & Destiny*:

"The pace began to heat up; employers like the railways, associations like the Chambers of Commerce and Rotary, vied with each other to set up camps"[2].

Serious incentive offers came on line. In Haryana the paving of access roads to villages and connection to the electricity supply became dependent on 'family planning' performance[3]. In another village a new well was provided in exchange for 100% participation of eligible couples in the family planning programme[4].

With the incentives came disincentives. Germaine Greer writes:

"In Bihar, all employees of the Department of Health & Family Planning had to motivate a certain number of acceptors for sterilisation under pain of censure, docked pay or, if the short-fall was of the order of 50% or more, dismissal"[5].

In June 1975 the Indian Supreme Court declared Mrs Ghandi's election invalid. She responded by declaring a State of Emergency under which all civil liberties were suspended. The sterilisation campaign could then proceed unchecked. Before the end of Emergency rule in 1977 6.5 million men had been vascectomised. 1774 people died as a direct consequence of the operation, and there is no doubt that many thousands more were sterilised against their will.

Racial tensions, never far below the surface in India, boiled over. There was intense hostility towards Muslims, who expressed the greatest reluctance to participate in the programme. As a result a police raid was carried out on Utta-var, a community of 8,000 Muslims who had refused to allow any family planning workers to enter the village. 550 men were rounded up and taken away. Of these 180 were forcibly sterilised[6]. This was far from being an isolated incident.

Western population lobbyists were delighted, not embarrassed, by the Indian government's performance. An analysis of the mass sterilisation campaign which appeared in *New Scientist* in 1977 revealed how "World Bank President Robert McNamara took time off his busy schedule during his Indian visit to call upon the Indian Health and Family Planning Minister to congratulate him for the Indian government's 'political will and determination' in popularizing family planning. This was during November 1976, at the height of the compulsory sterilization campaign"[7].

When the State of Emergency came to an end the Department of Family Planning was re-titled the Department of Family Welfare, and all talk of population control was replaced with references to mother and child health-care. However the programmes continued – and continue to the present day – much as before, except that the use of physical force has been ruled out.

A woman who appeared in the Channel 4 documentary *Something Like a War* explained:

"In my family the government decided how many children I'd have. We were very poor then and they said they'd withhold my husband's salary. What could we do without his salary?"[8]

As ever in the international population control movement, freedom of choice means choice for the planners, not the parents.

CHAPTER SEVEN

The Use of Force in China

"If there are people who seriously believe that there is not (coercion) in China, I can only answer what someone said when she saw the Duke of Wellington arm-in-arm with a Mrs Jones: 'Mr Jones I believe'. If you believe that, you will believe anything"

Lord Bauer, 1985[1]

The Chinese population control programme is undoubtedly the most famous in the world because of the fanaticism and the brutality with which the government's draconian measures have been carried out.

Following the Communist Revolution in 1949 there was no official recognition of any population problem in China. According to Chairman Mao, who regarded population control as a Western bourgeois measure for oppressing the proletariat, "Of all things in the world, people are the most precious"[2]. Mao believed that the successes of the socialist economy would eliminate any supposed problems of 'overpopulation', and in 1952 an editorial in the *People's Daily* described birth control as "a way of slaughtering the Chinese people without drawing blood".

Following the appalling tragedy of the "Great Leap Forward" between 1958 and 1961, when between 20 and 30 million people died in famines which followed the forced collectivisation of land, there was the familiar need for a scapegoat. Communism and Chairman Mao's great plan for the country could not be blamed: women who were supposedly having too many children were an easy target.

This is, in fact, one of the *leitmotifs* of population control. The supposed 'population explosion' is one of most welcome red herrings which was ever handed to politicians on a plate. It allows them to distract attention from the failure of their policies by diverting blame onto women. Mothers of large families become the scapegoats for politicians who are at a loss to account for the failure of their five year plans and their ten year plans – particularly as the control of fertility will allow the same politicians to abrogate even more power to themselves. People sometimes ask why population control appeals to politicians right across the political spectrum, from extreme right to extreme left. This is the reason.

Throughout the 1960s and 1970s the 'need' for population control was accepted by the Chinese government, and programmes were implemented. Initially the ideal was the three child family, which then came down to the two child family. In 1979, in the absence of any solutions to the inevitable problems of lack of economic growth which always accompany communism, the ideal number of children dropped to one.

The extraordinary idea of a nation of one-child families, in which people would soon have no brothers or sisters or aunts, uncles or cousins, caught the attention of the world's media. Soon, however, stories began to emerge concerning the brutally repressive measures which were being used to implement it.

In 1979 American sinologist Steven Mosher was able to take advantage of a thaw in U.S./Chinese diplomatic relations to obtain permission to spend a year living in a Chinese village. He had unprecedented access to ordinary Chinese people and was able to discover what life under communism was really like for them. This included the first opportunity for an impartial Western observer to see how the government was enforcing the one-child policy.

In the resulting book, *Broken Earth: The Rural Chinese*, Steven Mosher gave his eye-witness account of the methods which were being used to make women "think clear" about the population policy. He was able to join eighteen women, between five and nine months pregnant, who were rounded up by the local Communist Party cadre and taken to the commune headquarters where they were told they would be held until they agreed to abort their pregnancies. The women were left in no doubt as to their options:

"None of you has any choice in the matter. You must realise that your pregnancy affects everyone in the commune, and indeed affects everyone in the country"[3].

Mosher analyses the effectiveness of the approach:

"Alternately threatening and cajoling, persuading and reasoning, the cadres explain over and over why it is necessary to follow the Party line, applying a steady psychological pressure that deadens reason and gradually erodes the will to resist. Experience has taught the Chinese that arguing back at authority will only make matters worse, and so they listen passively and finally come to agree to whatever is being demanded of them"[4].

Partly as a result of the publication of Mosher's evidence, the U.S. delegation to the 1984 United Nations Population Conference in Mexico took a very stern line on abortion, insisting that it was not to be regarded as a method of family planning. The U.S. delegation also announced that it would not continue to fund organisations which were involved in any way with population programmes promoting abortion, as there was a strict prohibition of American taxpayers' money being used to fund abortions in other countries.

As a result of the subsequent investigation of the activities of some leading population groups, the United Nations Population Fund (UNFPA) and the International Planned Parenthood Federation (IPPF) were both warned that unless they ceased to fund the Chinese population programme they would lose all support from the U.S. government. They refused to give any such assurances and, in 1985, they lost the funding.

There have been numerous attempts since then to have the U.S. funding to these two key groups in the population lobby restored, on the basis that even if there were human rights abuses in the past, these have now been dealt with and the Chinese programme is now entirely voluntary.

In response to these claims China scholar John Aird undertook a thorough examination of all available evidence concerning the working of the Chinese programme. He combed through hundreds of articles in the government-controlled Chinese press, together with official directives, exhortations and policy documents which show what is really going on. He was able to translate the euphemisms (for example "remedial measures" for mandatory abortion) and to distinguish between versions for foreign consumption and instructions to the Communist Party cadres who actually carry out the policies. The resulting book, *The Slaughter of the Innocents: Coercive Birth Control in China* represents the most scholarly and exhaustive of all the studies which have been made of that subject. Most of the following account is based on Aird's work.

Aird was able to show that, in spite of the 'party line' being taken by Western population lobbyists, there had been no let-up by the Chinese authorities. The ferocity with which the one-child policy is enforced varies from year to year and from province to province, depending on other political factors, but there is certainly no freedom of choice for parents.

Nor has there ever been any known case of a party worker being disciplined for enforcing the policy too strictly. Indeed, how could there be, when party workers had been promised immunity from any such action by no less an authority than China's supreme leader, Deng Xiaoping. In 1981 he had been quoted by Chen Muhua, head of the family planning office under the State Council, as saying:

"In order to reduce the population use whatever means you must, but do it!" Chen added "With the support of the Party Central Committee you should have nothing to fear"[5].

Aird translates and reprints some of the official instructions to Communist Party cadres on the way in which the one-child policy was to be enforced:

"Those who insist on having a second or excessive birth must be treated according to the prescribed policies. If they are Party members or cadres, it is proposed that they be given Party and administrative discipline

"Birth control should be enforced . . . measures to reward good and punish evil should be implemented

"All newly married couples who are expecting must show their planned birth certificates. Those who are unable to produce a permit will have to undergo birth control measures (i.e. abortions)

"Illegal relationships (i.e. early marriages) which should be dissolved must be dissolved . . . those who are pregnant out of wedlock and have not reached the legal mariage age must undergo remedial operations (i.e. abortions)

"If an unauthorised baby is the second, third or subsequent child in a family and sterilisation has not been accepted, the family will be denied permission to build a dwelling, their water and electricity will be cut off . . . grain coupons will not be issued . . . drivers licenses and private business licenses will be revoked"[6]

Peer pressure has been brought to bear, *even on Chinese living in other countries*. In 1987 a Chinese couple receiving training in the USA who were expecting a second child received a letter from the population control office of their factory in China ordering the woman to have an abortion. She was warned that, if she refused:

" . . . our whole factory will be disqualified from any production contests, and the bonuses and benefits of all employees will be negatively affected . . . The consequences for you are unthinkable. You would be condemned by all the staff and line employees of the factory. How could you bear the losses you would cause and suffer?"[7]

In September 1991 *The Independent* published an article by Chinese journalist Liu Yin (not her real name, for obvious reasons) which reveals that the above threats are not empty. Liu Yin had been allowed to accompany a "task force" which was after eleven women with unauthorised pregnancies. Six had fled the village: the target was the other five. They were forcibly dragged from their houses in the middle of the night and taken to the county hospital:

"The families whose women escaped the raid were warned that if they did not go to the abortion centre within a week their houses would be pulled down. This was no bluff. On the way back from the raid, I saw six collapsed houses. No family in the village is allowed to provide shelter for the people whose houses have been destroyed . . .

"Hundreds of women – some more than six months pregnant – were packed in dark corridors and makeshift tents, waiting to be operated on in the 'abortion centre' in the hospital courtyard. Next to it was a public toilet. I went in: there was simply nowhere you could put your feet; it was filled with blood-soaked toilet paper. Behind the toilet stood a line of waste-bins: the aborted babies – some as old as eight months – were put there, then dumped somewhere else"[8].

The Chinese government-controlled media has been refreshingly open in its support for the use of coercion. In January 1989 a Beijing newspaper carried an article criticising those who advocated freedom of choice for individuals:

"We should justly and forcefully say that we must punish those who have turned a deaf ear to dissuasion from having additional children . . . and that suitable coercion should be implemented in China's family planning"[9].

This was followed in April by a report from the New China News Agency quoting an Agriculture Ministry official as saying that:

"Only coercive measures can be effective in alleviating the problems caused by the population explosion . . . From the perspective of future generations . . . temporary coercion is actually a philanthropic and wise policy"[10].

In August 1989 an article in a Shanghai social science journal claimed that:

". . . the coercive measures in the current population policy, such as knocking down houses, felling trees, confiscating . . . cattle, tractors and other large farm equipment" were "unscientific", whereas compulsory abortion was "entirely in accord with the spirit of the Constitution"[11].

John Aird, who quotes these examples in his book, explains:

"The writers were not recognized official spokesmen . . . but the fact that articles advocating coercion appeared openly in China's highly controlled press while no articles opposing coercion were permitted to appear is undoubtedly significant of the official attitude"[12].

SUPPORT FROM THE WEST

The most puzzling aspect of the Chinese population programme has not been its brutality: the history of the 20th century has taught us to appreciate the scale of the horrors which modern totalitarian governments can inflict. The most puzzling aspect has been the support which the programme has received from

Western individuals and groups which are committed to the principle of freedom of choice in reproductive matters.

David Bellamy, the TV naturalist and President of Population Concern, has praised the "Chinese model" as "a fantastic story of success . . . the Chinese understand the limitations of their environment and they have used that knowledge to *plan* for a healthy, well-fed population of sustainable size"[13], while the World Wide Fund for Nature (WWF) has praised the Chinese population programme as a "success story", citing its use of "group persuasion to change attitudes towards childbearing and family size"[14].

The most dramatic support, however, has come from IPPF and UNFPA, the two organisations which were prepared to face loss of U.S. government funding (amounting to over 25% of total revenues in IPPF's case) rather than stop supporting the Chinese programme. IPPF gives financial support at the rate of nearly US$1 million each year, but this pales into insignificance besides the UNFPA grant of US$57 million for the period 1990–1994.

Far from shunning the Chinese, the international population community has welcomed China into its midst. In 1983, when coercion in the Chinese programme was at an all time high, a U.N. Committee, with Rafael Salas, Executive Director of UNFPA as advisor, gave one of the first two U.N. population awards to Qian Xinzhong, the Minister-in-Charge of the State Family Planning Commission (SFPC) of China. When presenting the award U.N. Secretary-General Perez de Cuellar expressed "deep appreciation" for the way in which the Chinese had "marshalled the resources necessary to implement population policies on a massive scale"[15]. In the same year IPPF welcomed the Chinese Family Panning Association into full membership.

The Western support – both financial and moral – has been fully exploited by the Chinese goverment. The State Family Planning Commission was able to announce, in connection with the U.N. Award, that "This shows that the U.N. and the countries of the world approve of the achievements we have made"[16].

The appeal of the Chinese population control programme to the population lobby can easily be understood: on its own terms, it works. The total fertility rate has fallen from 5.8 children per woman in 1970 to 2.3 in 1990 – a truly staggering feat of social engineering. Since, with a population of around 1 billion people, the Chinese represent about a fifth of the world's population, any dramatic changes in fertility in China affect global trends.

This leaves unanswered the critical question: how do the international family planning/population control groups square support for the coercive Chinese programme with their frequently stated support for the principal of freedom of choice in matters of reproduction, and for the rights of women?

In attempting to answer this question we have to confront a paradox which lies at the heart of the population control movement.

CHAPTER EIGHT

Parents or the State?

"The claim by foreign family planners to respect the right of couples to determine freely the size of their families and the choice of contraceptive methods was put to its first test in China in the 1980s and failed. They sided with a brutally repressive regime against its people because it implemented their agenda. There is as yet no sign that that have learned anything sobering from this experience."

John Aird *The Slaughter of the Innocents: Coercive Birth Control in China*

The World Population Plan of Action, agreed at the U.N. World Population Conference in Bucharest in 1974, recognised "the basic human right of all couples and individuals to decide freely and responsibly the number and spacing of their children".

This sounds clear enough. There would certainly be no grounds here for government interference in the reproductive life of its citizens.

However there was an important qualification to the main principle. The WPPA goes on to state that "the responsiblity of couples and individuals in the excercise of this right takes into account the needs of their living and future children and their responsibilities towards the community".

In other words, this right is not a right at all. It can be overruled by the government, which decides on the type of reproductive behaviour which demonstrates a sense of "responsiblity towards the community". Presumably the goverment will also decide on the needs of future generations, whatever they may be.

The wording of the Bucharest declaration has been reproduced in most of the national and international declarations on the 'right' to family planning since 1974. It encapsulates that most important principal of population control: people cannot be left to do as they like.

The World Bank Report *Population Change and Economic Development* included a very clear statement concerning the rights of the individual *vis-a-vis* the state:

"Should governments not only ensure procreative freedom but also encourage social responsiblity? The answer in this Report is a firm yes . . .

A dilemma arises whenever pursuits of one set of values – improvement of material welfare through lower population growth, reduction of inequality, insurance of future security – threaten other values, such as freedom of choice and pronatalist customs and beliefs. But there is a balance between the private right of procreation and social responsiblity"[1].

Behaviour which is socially responsible will, of course, be decided by the state. If there is a conflict between the number of children people want to have and the number which the government – or the World Bank or the United Nations – wants them to have, the international family planning organisations can neatly sidestep the ethical dilemma by referring to the need to balance social needs against private preferences.

What this means in practice is that all of the fine words about freedom of choice do not add up to anything. There is certainly no guarantee that anyone from the Western population groups will come to the assistance of Third World parents who are being coerced, as experience has shown.

Coercion can, of course, take many forms. Anti-natalist propaganda can be coercive. It sets up tensions and anxieties with the aim of manipulating parents' decisions on family size by creating fear of public and peer group disapproval. The use of bribes and threats to force people to have fewer children than they would wish is certainly and obviously coercive. As the old saying goes, there are more ways than one to skin a cat, and there are more ways to coerce parents than by holding a woman down while she is aborted, or a man while he is vascectomised.

Even so, the notoriety of the Chinese government's one child per couple programme has put the population lobby on the spot. They have had to struggle hard with their words to justify supporting such a brutally coercive scheme.

John Aird has neatly encapsulated their verbal dexterity:

"In regard to the principle of reproductive freedom Mr Salas [Rafael Salas, Secretary General of the UNFPA] said that 'the relationship of the individual to the needs of society as a whole is a matter for each country to decide'[2] . . . In 1986 Mr Salas said that China's birth control practices were coercive by Western but not by Chinese standards[3] . . . In the same year Nafis Sadik, who succeeded Salas as head of the UNFPA, published an article in which she maintained that 'any limitations on the exercise of personal and voluntary choice of methods in [family planning] in itself represents a violation of the right to have access to family planning', but then she added that 'judgements about what constitutes free and informed choice must be made within the context of a particular culture and the context of the overall government programme for social and economic development'[4]

"These statements seem to imply that the definition of coercion is up to national governments, which negates the idea of universally applicable human rights in family planning. In effect, the UNFPA opposes coercion in principle but not in practice"[5].

It is even harder to tie down the International Planned Parenthood Federation which, like UNFPA, was prepared to lose its U.S government funding rather than withdraw support for the Chinese programme, and which also loudly proclaims its adherence to the principle of freedom of choice.

IPPF spokespersons seem to resolve the dilemma by denying that coercion takes place in China. Dr Pramilla Senanayake, who does media work for IPPF in the U.K., denied on *Newsnight* that the Chinese programme relied on compulsion:

"I wouldn't call it government compulsion – I think government support for those individuals to plan their family"[6].

She is also of the opinion that:

"In China . . . all methods of contraception are widely available . . . to the women and they have the choice to use them or not to use them . . . By and large the Chinese family planning programme is well spread out, available to all the masses that need to use it and without coercion"[7].

It is, of course, impossible to have a discussion about the ethics of supporting population programmes which rely on coercion when people do not admit that coercion takes place.

UNMET NEEDS

One of the key phrases which crops up again and again in population propaganda is 'unmet needs' – that is to say the need for family planning of those women who have no access to services. These unmet needs provide the justification for the ever-greater demands which population groups make for funding from public authorities.

References are frequently made to surveys such as the World Fertility Survey which was carried out by the World Health Organisation and published in the mid-1980s which, amongst other things, attempted to establish the number of women who wished to have no more children, or who had not planned their last pregnancy, and yet had no access to family planning. The figure of 300 million couples who are supposed to come into this 'unmet need' category is often cited.

In spite of the doom-laden jargon, meeting 'unmet needs' for contraception is easy. Providing birth control as a component of primary health care is both simple and cheap. As we mentioned above, there may be disagreements about the best methods to use, but governments which are in touch with the culture of their own people should have no difficulty in making family planning services universally available at minimal cost.

However, you can bring a horse to water but you can't make it drink. Birth control services may be made available but still not be used, for reasons which the studies cited on pages 10–11 make clear.

In these circumstances, the population controllers know the line to take: the people do not really understand their 'needs' at all. These 'needs' have to be pointed out to them by those who are more knowledgeable than they as to the number of children they should have.

An article on the Indian population programme which appeared in *People*, the magazine of the International Planned Parenthood Federation, made this plain. According to Vidya Pense, project manager for the Family Planning Association of India (FPAI):

> "They don't always perceive their needs. The welfare worker has to point them out"[8].

In the same article, a fieldworker who had been confronted by a father of two daughters who still wanted a son, concluded that:

> "It'll take a little more counselling to change his opinions"[9].

We can only speculate on the nature of the "counselling" which that poor man was going to receive. It is sad that, in India of all countries, family planners should have learned so little humility. They still think they know best what is good for other people. But then they are only repeating the lines they have learned from the rich and powerful organisations at the top of their movement. According to The World Bank:

> "To some extent family planning programs do more than simply satisfy unmet need ; they actually generate and then fill such need"[10].

What sort of 'need' is it which has to be generated by the very agency which is intending to fulfil it? Perhaps this 'unmet need' for family planning is akin to the 'unmet need' for a larger car, a jacuzzi bath or an expensive perfume – we don't realise we need these things until advertisers draw them to our attention.

It is clear that a need of which the supposed sufferers are unaware is not one which affects their lives in any serious way.

American economist Jacqueline Kasun takes the view that the 'unmet needs' of which the population controllers speak "are not those of the . . . poor for more birth control, but . . . their own for further control over the lives of people"[11].

CHAPTER NINE

Where were the feminists?

It is beyond doubt that population control programmes have infringed the human rights of Third World parents, particularly women. Couples have been subjected to intolerable pressures, through government propaganda, through threats and bribes, through peer group pressure and in other ways, to have fewer children than they want.

In extreme cases, such as China and India in the mid-1970s, population programmes have even had recourse to the use of physical force.

Throughout the period in which the population control movement has been extending its influence, we have also witnessed the rise of a powerful force which has had a dramatic impact on social policy: feminism.

The feminist goal has been to end the oppression of women by men. Feminists demand equal treatment for women, and at the top of their agenda has been the issue of reproductive freedom. They have demanded, successfully in many countries, that women should be able to control their fertility through access to contraception and abortion.

'Freedom of choice' has been the feminist legend. Pro-abortion campaigners describe themselves as being 'pro-choice'.

It is difficult to understand, therefore, why feminists have had almost nothing to say about the coercion of their Third World sisters through population programmes. If the freedom to choose really means anything, it should mean the freedom to choose to have a large family as well as a small family, or no children at all.

American author Stephen Trombley recounted the history of the movement for the coercive sterilisation of those judged unfit to 'breed' in his book *The Right to Reproduce*. He dealt partly with the population control movement, but mainly with the widespread abuse of women through coercive sterilisation in Western countries like America up until the 1970s. In his summary to the book he raised the question of why the feminists had done so little to prevent or expose the abuses:

> "One explanation may be that the movement did not want to divert time and energy away from abortion, which was considered to be *the* issue. Perhaps it was felt that by arguing for one right (access to medical services) at the same time that one was arguing for another (an end to medical victimization), the case for abortion would be weakened"[1].

Stephen Trombley's argument would hold equally true with regard to population control. The population control movement has been the principal engine for making abortion services easily available around the world. When Western population groups move into Third World countries they start to agitate for the repeal of laws restricting access to abortion or, in some cases, they just set up the abortion clinics anyway without bothering to change the law. For some feminists, the attempted universal provision of abortion through population control has taken precedence over making known the abuses to which women are being subjected under these programmes.

This is the only conceivable explanation for the way in which feminists have not only turned a blind eye to population control, but have often allowed their movement to be used as the very means for promoting it.

Because of the determination to avoid charges of racism and imperialism (*see page 8 above*) population control programmes are habitually carried out in the name of health care for mothers and their children. This allows them to be brought under the heading of Women's Issues, or even Women's Rights. Population control activists have been able to ride into Third World countries on the back of feminist rhetoric, although it is difficult to see how women's rights are served by taking decisions on family size away from women and vesting them in politicians (who are usually men).

In 1985 the United Nations held its End-of-Decade-for-Women Conference in Nairobi. Feminists from around the world participiated in the discussions on women's issues which evinced little agreement on any point – apart from the need for population control. The siting of the conference in Nairobi was significant because Kenya was said at the time to have the highest birthrate in the world, at eight children per woman, and had become a particular target for population activities. Within weeks of the conference ending, President Moi announced that four children would the maximum number permitted for Kenyan women, and that any parents going over that would be subject to a number of penalties, including the withdrawal of free primary education.

Like many policies announced by African leaders, there is no evidence that this was ever put into effect. However, it provides an interesting example of the way in which policies which oppress women can actually benefit from the support of feminist activism.

The next United Nations conference on Women is to take place in 1995 – in China.

CHAPTER TEN

More Threats

As those who oppose the implementation of population policies know, dealing with the arguments for population control is like shooting at a moving target.

The basis for the programmes keeps changing. In the 1960s population growth was supposed to be threatening us with mass famines. In fact food production has kept so far ahead of population growth rates that there is now more food in the world per head of population than ever before.

It was then said that population growth would cause poverty and slow up economic development. Even the President of the World Bank, an organisation long committed to population control, now has to admit:

> "The evidence is clear that economic growth in excess of population growth rates can be achieved and maintained by both developed and developing countries"[1].

We then had the scare stories that natural resources were running out. Some enthusiastic population lobbyists even put dates on the expiry of certain important resources. Convinced that resources were becoming more available, not more scarce, American economist Julian Simon made a bet with population scaremonger Paul Ehrlich on the availability of resources as measured by price. They bet on the value of $1,000 worth of five resources over a period of ten years. If prices went up in real terms (after allowing for inflation) Simon would pay Ehrlich the difference; if they went down, Ehrlich would pay Simon.

The bet expired at the end of 1990, by which time the original $1,000 worth of resources could have been bought for $424. So much for scarcity.

The arguments for population control have now moved on to the supposed damage to the environment which population growth causes. However, the aim of population control programmes remains the same whichever rationale is used. In an article on population policies in Africa which appeared in *People*, the magazine of the International Planned Parenthood Federation, John May, a senior demographer with the Futures Group in Washington, asked:

> "Which rationale should be used to promote family planning: the health line of reasoning or demographic, economic or even environmental arguments?"[2].

Clearly it makes little difference, because the policies are going to be the same.

There is, however, one very significant difference between the 'traditional' arguments for population control – famine, poverty etc – and the new 'environmental' ones. Earlier policies were promoted on the assumption – however mistaken – that they would help human beings to achieve a reasonable material standard of living. The new environmental or Green arguments follow a different line. They promote the idea that human beings are spoiling the planet by their activities; that human needs are being satisfied at the expense of the 'needs' of other species; that human beings are not necessarily more important than other species; and that the rest of the planet might be better off if there were fewer of us. According to a book published for the World Wide Fund for Nature:

> "We must halt human population growth not just to insure the well-being of humanity but to restore the interdependent biotic community in which we human beings must learn to see ourselves as members not masters"[3].

Eliciting concern for the human rights of women who are pressured to restrict their families in the interests of government policy has proved difficult. Even Amnesty International, which has done extensive work in revealing the abuses of women's rights in Tibet, has been unwilling to deal with reports of forced abortions under the occupying Chinese government's population programme.

There will be even less concern for the rights of Third World parents when human rights themselves begin to move down the scale in relation to the rights of other species, or "the biotic community". This is in fact what has been happening with the development of the movement campaigning for animal rights, and even plant rights. Human beings have come to be widely regarded as nothing special in the order of creation. According to Dr M S Swaminthan, former President of the International Union for the Conservation of Nature:

> "Unless the penguin and the poor evoke from us equal concern, conservation will be a lost cause"[4].

It is not uncommon for Greens to speak of people as a form of pollution, or even a cancer of the face of the earth[5]. The eagerness to reduce human numbers has led to a resurgence of the crude threats which characterised the pronouncements of Kingsley Davis and Bernard Berelson. According to *A Green Manifesto* by Sandy Irvine and Alec Ponton, which is recommended reading for Green Party members:

> ". . . help given to regimes opposed to population policies is counter-productive and should cease. They are the true enemies of life and do not merit support. So too are those religions which do not actively support

birth control. Green governments would reluctantly have to challenge head-on such damaging beliefs"[6].

Irvine and Ponton quote with approval the view of environmentalist Garrett Hardin that:

"Freedom is divisible. If we want to keep the rest of our freedoms, we must restrict the freedom to breed"[7].

If the rights of individual women to freedom of choice are to be superceded not only by the supposed national interest, but also by the rights of 'the planet' or 'the biotic community', then the outlook for reproductive freedom is bleak indeed.

CHAPTER ELEVEN

Trust the Parents

"The children who are born are generally desired. Children at any rate are avoidable. To deny this is to suggest that parents in less developed countries procreate without an understanding of the consequences or without the will or the sense of responsiblity to prevent them. This view treats people of the less developed world with altogether unwarranted condescension or contempt"

Professor Lord Bauer, *Equality, the Third World and Economic Delusion*[1]

"The birth of every unwanted child is a tragedy, for itself and for the unwilling parents, but in spite of all the attention we have given to the matter, more unwanted children are born to us, the rich, than to them, the poor"

Germaine Greer *Sex and Destiny*[2]

The population control movement is fired by a strange witches' brew of idealism, selfishness and fear.

There is no doubt that many of its key activists, together with a large section of the supporters at grass roots level, are motivated by a genuine desire to improve the health of Third World women by giving them access to Western contraceptive technology.

There is also the selfishness of those who, consciously or subconsciously, feel that growing numbers of people in the developing countries may represent a challenge to the supremacy of the West.

Finally there is the fear that population growth may be one of the factors propelling us towards an environmental holocaust which will leave the earth uncomfortable for us and perhaps uninhabitable for future generations.

It is clearly impossible, in a monograph of this size, to deal with all of the serious issues with which population growth has been connected. It is enough to say here that we must acknowledge these fears to be real enough to the people who express them. Many, no doubt, would say that they deplore the fact that Third World parents have to be denied the sort of freedom of choice in matters of family size which we in the West take for granted, but that this is the lesser of two evils. They regard Third World parents rather as some parents regard their children – well-meaning but so irresponsible that they have to be restrained from behaving in such a way as to damage themselves and others.

Fundamental to this view is the assumption that Third World parents are unable to control their own fertility, and that government planners would make a better job of doing it for them. Both of these assumptions are fundamentally flawed.

There is a considerable body of anthropological evidence to suggest that peoples in different cultures at different times have always regulated their fertility, using a variety of traditional means such as breastfeeding, post-partum abstinence and *coitus interruptus*. It does not all depend on having access to the latest Western contraceptive technology. Furthermore, as Germaine Greer argues in her book *Sex and Destiny*, by rushing Western contraception, which is the product of Western culture, onto what she calls traditional societies, we may be disrupting or even destroying the cultural mechanisms which regulate fertility in Third World countries. This could result in unwanted pregnancies, the elimination of which is the very aim of family planning.

Parents take into account a variety of factors when deciding on how many children they wish to have. They consider their own circumstances, of course, as well as the sort of society in which they are living. Factors such as educational and employment opportunities for their offspring are usually included in these calculations.

The reason that women in India have more children than women in Islington is not because they do not have access to contraception. They do. The reason is is because they live in cultures which carry different assumptions about marriage, the family and childbearing. A traditional greeting for an Indian bride is "May you be the mother of eight sons". This is a contingency against which most Western wives would wish to insure themselves!

The British population group Marie Stopes International operates from a house in Whitfield Street which was bequeathed by Marie Stopes herself to the Eugenics Society. Its Georgian door and fanlight, characteristic of London townhouses of the period, are reproduced on the front of MSI clinics around the world to symbolise the way in which, in the view of the clinics' promoters, "the familiar MSI door opens onto life"[3].

It would appear that no one at MSI has considered the possibility that, to an Indian slum-dweller, a Georgian door and fanlight might also symbolise a foreign culture with alien values.

PARENTS OR PLANNERS?

Those who advocate population control do not trust parents. They prefer to put their trust in government planners, or international bureaucrats at the

United Nations or the World Bank. These people are supposed to be able to decide how many children parents in Third World countries should have more wisely than the Third World parents themselves.

Of all the foolish confidences which have been placed in the wisdom of central planning, this must be one of the most absurd. How can a politician or a U.N. official believe that he (or she) comprehends the peasant woman's needs better than she does herself? The politicians would no doubt answer that they have the best interests of the country at heart, and that they must plan for a nation whereas parents work on the more limited horizons of family needs.

In the real world we now have ample evidence that centrally planned economies are wasteful, corrupt and inefficient. With the collapse of communism in the Eastern bloc and the almost universal acceptance of market economies, it seems hardly necessary to argue this point.

Why should the planners think they know more about other people's reproductive needs than they knew about their economic behaviour? Their failure in the one sphere is likely to be every bit as complete as their failure in the other has been shown to have been. It is a failure which carries greater penalties for those who pay the costs, however, because family life and the rearing of children constitute, for most people, their main chance of happiness. Better to be poor than childless – particularly in the underdeveloped economies of the Third World, with no pension funds and no financial institutions to allow people to invest for the future. In those circumstances, children are your pension – your guarantee against an old age of poverty and loneliness.

As the developing countries modernise, or Westernise (the terms are interchangable), it is quite likely that parents will begin to imitate First World norms in family size, as they obtain access to universal health care and education, unemployment benefit and pension funds, and the whole rainbow spectrum of exciting choices and opportunities which science and technology offer us.

To coerce Third World parents into taking only one part of the package – the preference for small families or no children at all – without getting the rest is to force them to pay the bill before they have taken delivery of the goods.

THE ROLE OF THE STATE

Perhaps the fundamental question, with regard to population programmes, is the relationship between the state and its citizens. This is core issue, the one which underlies any discussion on population, whether it concerns food output, scarcity of resources, energy policy or the environment.

Do you think that governments and other outside bodies should have the power to coerce people in the most private areas of their lives?

Those who believe in the wisdom and beneficence of planners and politicians may say yes. Those who take a more sceptical view, and regard those in the public sector as every bit as self-interested as private citizens, will say no.

Those with reservations about population control programmes regard the institutions of the state as being in existence to serve their families – not the other way around. Given the choice between trusting parents and trusting government planners, they would chose the parents every time. Of course, parents may make mistakes, but they will bear the cost of those mistakes, because in every culture parents shoulder the main burden of bringing up their children. They are unlikely to make the same mistake twice.

Government planners, on the other hand, need never face the consequences of their failed programmes. On the contrary, when they fail – as they must, because population control will never solve the problems it purports to tackle – this failure will provide the justification for strengthening their own powers and increasing the severity of the policies.

THE NEED TO SPEAK PLAINLY

Finally, it would be of the greatest assistance in the public discussion of population policies if those promoting them would observe a more exact use of terminology.

The term family planning should not be used to describe schemes which are designed to pressure people into having fewer children than they would wish to have. These are more properly designated by the term population control.

If Western governments are determined to use their taxpayers' money to finance programmes which do not respect the freedom of choice of individual couples then they should, at least, make clear the nature of the programmes to the people who are paying for them.

References

Introduction
(1) Malcolm Potts, "Turning dreams into reality", *People* Vol 16 No 4 1989

Chapter One:
(1) Kingsley Davis "Population Policy: Will Current Programs Succeed?" *Science* Vol 158 10 November 1967, p.738.
(2) *ibid.* p.733
(3) *ibid.* p. 734 & 733
(4) *ibid.* p.734
(5) *ibid.* p.738
(6) Bernard Berelson "Beyond Family Planning", a paper given to the International Family Planning Conference , Dacca, 28 January–4 February 1969
(7) N C Wright speaking at the CIBA symposium *Man & his Future* ed. Wolstenholme, London 1963
(8) *The Times*, Letters to the Editor, 30 July 1990
(9) Peter Godwin "Inside Nairobi" *The Sunday Times* 23 March 1986
(10) For a full account of NSSM 200 and its reception see *Population Control & National Security: A Review of U.S. National Security Policy* published by Information Project for Africa Inc, PO Box 43345, Washington D.C. 20010, 1991
(11) *St Louis Post-Dispatch* 22 April 1977 p.1

Chapter Two:
(1) Sally Mugabe "High Fertility Hampers Women's Status" *Popline* June 1987. *Popline* is a publication of the World Population News Service.
(2) Information Project for Africa, *Unconventional Warfare and the Theory of Competitive Reproduction*, Working Paper No 2, IPFA Foreign Policy Series, Washington 1991, pp.31–33
(3) Family Planning Operations Research Sub-Projects, Columbia University/TVT Associates
(4) Francine van del Walle and Baba Traore "Attitudes of Women and Men Towards Contraception in a Town in Burkina Faso", *Fertility Determinants Research Notes* No 14, The Population Council, New York, December 1986
(5) Agency for International Development, Sub-Project Paper, Family Health Initiatives II – Nigeria, 9 July 1987. AID document facility no. PD–AAW-850. See pp.6 & 8
(6) *The State of African Demography*, International Union for the Scientific Study of Population, Liege, Belgium, 1988 pp.31 & 38
(7) John C Caldwell and Pat Caldwell in *Population Growth and Reproduction in Sub-Saharan Africa*, The World Bank, Washington 1990
(8) Roushdie A Henin, "An assessment of Kenya's Family Planning Program:

1975–1979", published in *Population, Aid and Development – Proceedings of an International Meeeting on Aid and Cooperation in the Field of Population and Development: Issues and Strategies*, International Union for the Scientific Study of Population, Liege, Belgium, 1985

(9) The World Bank *Population Change & Economic Development*, reprinted from *The World Development Report 1984* OUP 1985 p.94

(10) Barber Conable "Choices for a better life" *People* Vol 17 No 2 1990 p.4

(11) Jean M Guilfoyle "Laying Foundations for Abortion Policy" *Population Research Institute Review* Vol 2 No 1 Jan/Feb 1992

(12) Robert A Levine "Maternal Behavior and Child Development in High Fertility Populations" *Fertility Determinants Research Notes No 2* Population Council September 1984

(13) *Fertility Determinants Research Notes No 3* December 1984

Chapter Three:

(1) Kinglsey Davis *op.cit.* p.733

(2) Eric Siegel, "Memorable Messages", *The Baltimore Sun*, 12 November 1991

(3) Phyllis Piotrow "Sing and the world sings with you", People, Vol 16 No 3 1989

(4) Christopher Walker "Soap operas sing praises of birth control in Egypt", *The Times*, 22 May 1991

(5) Agency for International Development Cooperative Agreement No.DPE-3004-A-00-6057-00 1 September 1986

(6) Agency for International Development Project contract no.620-0001-C-8013-00, 15 March 1988, estimated total cost $14,998,497

(7) Information Project for Africa *Unconventional Warfare and the Theory of Competetive Reproduction*, Working Paper No 2 IPFA Foreign Policy Series, Washington DC, 1991, p.50

(8) From Dr Mahler's address to the IPPF Members' Assembly in Ottowa, November 1989, reported in *People* Vol 17 No 1 1990

(9) Peter Bauer *Population Growth: Curse or Blessing?*, Centre for Independent Studies, Australia, 1990 p.15

Chapter Four:

(1) Joachim Weller "A Vertical approach in Vietnam", *People*, Vol 16 No 1 1989

(2) John Cleland and W Parker Mauldin "The Promotion of Family Planning by Financial Payments: The case of Bangladesh", *Studies in Family Planning* Vol 22 No 1 Jan/Feb 1991

(3) *ibid.*

(4) *Population Headliners* published by the Population Division of the United Nations Economic and Social Commission for Asia and the Pacific (ESCAP), Thailand, April 1991

(5) Hilary Standing and Betsy Hartmann *Food, Saris and Sterilisation: Population Control in Bangladesh*, Bangladesh International Action Group, London, 1985

(6) The World Bank, *Population Change & Economic Development*, extracted from *World Development Report 1984*, published Oxford University Press, 1985 pp.84/85

(7) *ibid.* p.85

(8) Bauer *op.cit.* p.3

(9) *World Development Report 1980*, The World Bank, Washington 1980, p.80

(10) The Population Council, *Studies in Family Planning* Vol 5 No 5 May 1974 pp.148–151 and Vol 7 No 7 July 1976 pp.188–196

(11) The Population Council *Studies in Family Planning* Vol 9 No 9 September 1978 pp.235–237; Select Committee on Population, *Report* "Population & Development Assistance", U.S. House of Representatives, 95th Congree, 2nd Session. Washington, U.S. Government Printing Office 1978, p.70

(12) S Surjaningrat and R H Pardoko "Review of some of the management aspects of the Indonesian Population and Family Planning Programme", Technical Report Series of the National Family Planning Coordination Board, Monograph no 37, Indonesia, 1983 p.3

(13) The World Bank *Population Change & Economic Development op.cit.* p.31

(14) Ninuk Widyantoro "Complete reproductive health care in Indonoesia", *People* Vol 16 No 4 1989 p.21

(15) Seclect Committee on Population *op.cit.* p.68

(16) Margot Cohen "New Strategies in Indonesia" *People* Vol 18 No 2 p.13

(17) *Something Like A War* Produced by D & N Productions in association with Equal Media Ltd (London). Shown on Channel 4 13 April 1992

(18) Kabra S G & Narayanan R "Sterilisation camps in India" *The Lancet* Vol 335 Jan 27 1990

(19) *ibid.*

(20) The World Bank *op.cit.* p.83

Chapter Five:

(1) The World Bank *op.cit.* p.107

(2) James F Phillips et al "Integrating Health Service Components into a Comprehensive Family Planning and Basic MCH Programme; Lessons from the MATLAB Family Planning Health Services Project", paper presented at the National Council for International Health Conference on International Health & Family Planning: Controversy and Consensus, Washington 10–13 June 1984.

(3) *ibid.* p.8

(4) Marjorie A Koblinsky et al "Barriers to Implementing an Effective National MCH-FP Program", paper presented at the 11th Annual International Health Conference, Arlington, Virginia, 11–13 June 1984, p.4

(5) Family Education Trust *The Great Population Hoax,* video, 1986

(6) "Invest in women, UNFPA tells governments" *People* Vol 16 No 3 1989 p.31

(7) The World Bank *op.cit.* p.107

(8) IMCH Newsletter Vol 18 No 189 Jan/Feb 1991

(9) Margot Cohen "New Strategies in Indonesia" *People* Vol 18 No 2 1991

Chapter Six:

(1) Meredith Minkler "Consultants or colleagues: the role of the U.S. population advisers in India" *Population & Development Review* December 1971

(2) Germaine Greer *Sex & Destiny*, Secker & Warburg 1984, p.351. Dr Greer's account of the Indian government's sterilisation campaign, from which most of this information has been extracted, occurs in the chapter "Governments as Family Planners".

(3) Nancy S Henley and Sagar C Jain *Family Planning in Haryana: Evaluation of a State Program in India*, Chapel Hill 1977 p.13

(4) Robert M Veatch "Governmental Population Incentives: Ethical Issues at Stake" *Studies in Family Planning* vol 8 no 4 April 1977 pp.100–108

(5) V A Pai Pandaniker, R N Bishnoi and O P Sharma *Family Planning Under the Emergency: Policy Implications of Incentives and Disincentives*, New Delhi 1979, quoted in Germaine Greer *op.cit.* p.355

(6) *Shah Commission of Enquiry Third and Final Report* 6 August 1978
(7) J Hanlon and A Agrawal "Mass Sterilisation at Gunpoint" *New Scientist*, London, 5 May 1977
(8) *Something Like A War* Channel 4 13 April 1992

Chapter Seven:
(1) ed. Ben Wattenberg and Karl Zinmeister *Are World Population Trends a Problem?*, American Enterprise Institute, Washington, 1985 pp.45/46
(2) Sun Jingzhi "Eliminate the Worship-America Ideology in the Field of Geography" *RMRB*, Beijing, 2 August 1952
(3) Steven W. Mosher *Broken Earth: The Rural Chinese*, Collier MacMillan, London, 1983 p.226
(4) *ibid.* p.229/230
(5) John S Aird *The Slaughter of the Innocents: Coercive Birth Control in China*, American Enterprise Institute, Washington, 1990,p.82
(6) *ibid.* pp.45, 47, 48, 66, 71/2
(7) *ibid.* p.75
(8) Liu Yin (not real name) "China's wanted children", *The Independent* 11 September 1991
(9) Xie Zhenjiang "There is no route of retreat" *JJRB* 24 January 1989, FBIS, No 30, February 15 1989 p.37
(10) *Fourth and Last of Population Series* pp.52–53
(11) Kuang Ke, "Some Suggestions on Legislating Childbirths", *Social Sciences*, Shanghai, No 8, 15 August 1989 pp.35–37
(12) John Aird *op.cit.* p.84
(13) David Bellamy, Foreward to ed.Norman Myers *The Gaia Atlas of Planet Management* Pan Books 1985 p.10
(14) WWF News May/June 1990
(15) "Perez de Cuellar issues warning on overpopulation", *Popline* Vol 5 No 9 October 1983 p.4
(16) State Family Planning Commission "Take the Chinese road to family planning work", *Health Gazette Family Planning Edition*, 28 September 1984 p.1

Chapter Eight:
(1) The World Bank *op.cit.* p.16
(2) Raphael M Salas "Population Assistance is Here toStay", *Populi* Vol 12 No 4 1985 p.6
(3) Remarks to a public form in Washington sponsored by the Population Institute 8 April 1986
(4) Nafis Sadik "The Importance of Voluntarism" *Populi* Vol 13 No 4 1986 pp.17 & 22
(5) John Aird *op.cit.* pp.113/114
(6) *Newsnight* BBC TV 22 April 1992
(7) *Gloria Live* BBC TV, 15 May 1990
(8) Bishakha Datta "Focusing on Women in Karnataka" *People* Vol 18 No 2 1991 pp.6–8
(9) *ibid.*
(10) The World Bank *Population Change and Economic Development op. cit.* p.94
(11) Jacqueline Kasun *The War Against Population* Ignatius Press, San Francisco 1988 p.207

Chapter Nine:
(1) Stephen Trombley *The Right to Reproduce: A History of Coercive Sterilisation* Weidenfeld and Nicolson, London, 1988 p.254

Chapter Ten:
(1) Speech by Barber Conable, President of the World Bank, to the IPPF Members' Assembly, Ottowa, November 1989. An edited version of the speech appeared in *People* Vol 17 No 2 1990
(2) John May "A new wave of population policies" *People* Vol 18 No 1 1991 p.8
(3) Frances Moore Lappe and Rachel Schurman *Taking Population Seriously* A WWF book published by Earthscan, London, 1989 p.14/15
(4) quoted in *Earthwatch* No 41 1991 p.18. *Earthwatch* was an environmental supplement to *People*, published by IPPF, London
(5) The human race is compared to an infectious disease in *The Gaia Peace Atlas* ed. Frank Barnaby Pan 1988 p.111 and to a "super-malignancy on the face of the planet" in *The Gaia Atlas of Planet Management* ed. Norman Myers Pan 1985 p.20
(6) Sandy Irvine and Alec Ponton *A Green Manifesto*, Macdonald Optima, 1988 p.23
(7) *ibid.* p.22

Chapter Eleven:
(1) P T Bauer *Equality, the Third World and Economic Delusion*, Methuen, London, 1982 p.63
(2) Germaine Greer *Sex and Destiny*, Secker and Warburg, 1984 p.418
(3) Marie Stopes International *Can we redeem our planet without it costing the earth?* pamphlet, London, undated.

APPENDIX: EXAMPLE OF PROPOSED MEASURES TO REDUCE U.S. FERTILITY BY UNIVERSALITY OR SELECTIVITY OF IMPACT

Universal impact	Selective impact depending on socio-economic status
Social Constraints	*Economic Deterrents/Incentives*
Restructure family:	Modify tax policies:
a) Postpone or avoid marriage	a) Substantial marriage tax
b) Alter image of ideal family	b) Child tax
Compulsory education of children	c) Tax married more than single
	d) Remove parents' tax exemptio
Encourage increased homo-sexuality	e) Additional taxes on parents with more than one or two children in school
Educate for family limitation Fertility control agents in water supply	Reduce/eliminate paid maternity leave or benefits
Encourage women to work	Reduce/eliminate children's or family allowances
	Bonuses for delayed marriages an greater child-spacing
	Pensions for women of 45 with less than N children
	Eliminate welfare payments after first two children
	Chronic Depression

The author of this chart was Frederick S. Jaffé Vice President of Planned Parenthood/World Population

54

	Measures predicated on existing motivation to prevent unwanted pregnancy
equire women to work and ovide few child care facilities	Payments to encourage sterilization
mit/eliminate public financed edical care, scholarships, using, loans and subsidies to milies with more than N children	Payments to encourage contraception
	Payments to encourage abortion
cial Controls	Abortion and sterilization on demand
ompulsory abortion of out-of-edlock pregnancies	Allow certain contraceptives to be distributed non-medically
ompulsory sterilization of all ho have two children except for a w who would be allowed three	Improve contraceptive technology
onfine childbearing to only a nited number of adults	Make contraception truly available and accessible to all
ock certificate-type permits for ildren	Improve maternal health care, with family planning as a core element
ousing Policies	
Discouragement of private home ownership	
Stop awarding public housing based on family size	

Source: "Activities Relevant to the Study of Population Policy for the U.S." Memorandum, from Frederick S. Jaffé to Bernard Berelson, March 11, 1969. Originally printed in *Family Planning Perspectives*, October 1970.

ABOUT THE AUTHOR

ROBERT WHELAN was educated at the John Fisher School, Purley and Trinity College, Cambridge, where he read English. He has written and produced a series of educational videos for the Family Education Trust on medical and social issues including *The Truth About AIDS, The Three Rs of Family Life, The Great Population Hoax* and *Facing Facts on Population*. He is the Director (UK) of the Committee on Population & The Economy which was formed, under the international chairmanship of Julian Simon, to carry out and disseminate research into population issues. He is the author of *Mounting Greenery*, which was published by the Education Unit of the Institute for Economic Affairs, and he has spoken and broadcast widely on population.